Interview *with* Death

A Handbook to the Hereafter

Loretta J. Poisson

Illustrations by Linda "iLham" Barto

For Ordering, Please Contact
Kitab House, Inc.
www. KitabHouse.com
(404) 585- 8177

amana publications

First Edition
(1431AH/2010AC)

© Copyright 1431AH/2010AC
amana publications
10710 Tucker Street
Beltsville, Maryland 20705-2223 USA
Tel: (301) 595-5999 / Fax: (301) 595-5888
E-mail: amana@igprinting.com
Website: www.amana-publications.com

Library of Congress Cataloging-in-Publication Data

Poisson, Loretta.
  Interview with death : a handbook to the hereafter / Loretta Poisson.
    p. cm.
  ISBN 978-1-59008-062-7
  1. Death--Religious aspects--Islam. 2. Death--Religious aspects--Islam--Koranic teaching.
I. Title.
  BP166.815.P65 2010
  297.2'3--dc22
                          2010020487

DEDICATION

*By the Will of God I conceived this book,
and I dedicate it to Him in all of His Glory.
May it be a constant reminder for myself and all
who venture into its pages with the sole purpose
of improving their relationship with Him.*

INTRODUCTION

THIS GUIDE TO THE HEREAFTER started out to be a personal day-to-day reminder for me during the month of Ramadan 2009. Being Muslim, I knew that frequent remembrance of death, the grave, and the Day of Judgment would be of value to one trying to stay on the straight path, and what better way, I mused, than to put myself there and see for myself. I have read many books and internet articles and listened to a variety of scholars who referenced the Holy Qur'an and the sayings of Prophet Muhammed chronicling the journey to Heaven or Hell, and after many years, I was actually visualizing these scenes quite clearly, so when I sat down before Ramadan to write what was in my head, it flowed like water from a jug. When I did the first reread I said, "Oh, this is just too valuable not to share!"

This project strengthened my faith, and I hope that the reader will use the guide the way I did, i.e., when times got tough, or when I leaned a little too far from the path, I would read whichever part would bring me back to center. Part 1 starts with Death and Illness and takes the reader through to Paradise. Part 2 begins with the same theme, Death and Illness, but then takes the reader through to the Hellfire. Nearly all of this information is sourced from, and in accordance with, the Islamic tradition. No matter who you are or what your religion, I need to point out here that everyone, Muslim or non-Muslim, who is seeking to improve his life on earth and in the Hereafter can benefit from these stories. Try to picture yourself in both of these scenarios, and hopefully it will shift your heart. I tried not to take too broad of an approach or take too much 'literary liberty' and stuck to the Qur'an and sayings of the Prophet, but some expansion was necessary to bring the picture to light, and bring it down to a more personal level. I believe this book gives us a human view of something we can only imagine – the true reality being too far out of our grasp.

God Almighty in the Qur'an says in Chapter 4 Verse 78, "Wherever you are, Death will find you out, even if you are in towers built up strong and high!" Death is undeniably certain, and Islam is not the first religion to state this.

For example, even the ancient Egyptian civilization was based on religion, and rebirth after death was its main focus. This belief, possibly a remnant of an earlier prophetic time, guided the Egyptian funeral practices; there are numerous scenes on the tomb walls of the judgment in the Afterlife. Getting your reward there meant coming with a sinless heart and in their beliefs, that heart would be put on one side of a scale and the 'Shu feather of truth and justice' taken from the headdress of the goddess Ma'at would be put on the other. If the heart weighed less than the feather, the person passed through and received the reward of the Afterlife, but if the heart weighed more, they would be immediately devoured by a demon waiting underneath.

Traditional Judaism also had the idea of life after death and the belief in the concept of Heaven and Hell, and a summary from the School of Shammai reflects that. It says there will be three groups on the Day of Judgment, one of righteous people, one of the wicked, and one in between. The righteous will be given eternal life in Heaven, the wicked, eternal life in Hell, and the third will go to Hell and plead until they are saved. *"And I will bring the third part through the fire and will refine them as silver is refined, and will try them as gold is tried. They shall call on My name and I will answer them"* (Zechariah 13:9)

The Bible also speaks about two very different outcomes of eternal life, but they are mostly spoken of metaphorically: A city of gold in Heaven and a river of fire in Hell.

In contrast, the process of death and the impending Afterlife in Islam is not only clearly spelled out in the Qur'an and sayings of the Prophet; it is repeated over and over again for emphasis. We don't have to guess what our outcome will be; we only need take to heart the vivid reminders on nearly every page of the Qur'an. I have tried to create my own interpretation of those reminders with this guide, and I hope that certainty of the Afterlife settles into your hearts as it has settled into mine, turning your gaze upward and changing your aspirations in this life forever.

I want to sincerely acknowledge the accomplished illustrations done by Linda "iLham" Barto. I believe they intertwine beautifully with the text, and add a dimension I could never have put into words.

I pray that God Almighty guides us all by whatever means He deems best to our final destination, Paradise and eternal life in His loving radiance. *Ameen,* may it be so.

Loretta J. Poisson

PARADISE

Inheritance of a Noble Heart

ILLNESS BEFORE DEATH AND THE AGONY OF DEATH

Be sure that We shall test you with something of fear and hunger, some loss in goods, lives, and the fruits of your toil…
[Qur'an, 2: 155]

11

… I SEEM TO BE DRIFTING on a vast blue ocean. It is peaceful, calm, and filled with contentment. Suddenly I am pulled back as my husband's hand slips into mine and the pain of my illness screams through me like a shot of acid through my veins. "Please say the Shahada," my husband gently prods. "Please!" I form the words, barely a whisper now, "I believe there is no god but God and Muhammed is His messenger," and this manifest is like honey on my searing tongue. I know I must do this while my soul is still in my body; when it reaches the throat, called gharghara, then it is too late, my life is over. The compassionate tears I see tumbling down my husband's face pain me as much as the ailment God has allowed to consume my flesh. A person can live a few seconds or a hundred years; my life split the difference. I have quickly learned that death is a process and not an event. As I savor the final touch of his hand in mine, all the fears around dying come rushing in. I remember the grave and the stark solitude, the scarring of these moments on my husband's heart, fear that the pain will make me heedless of God in these final precious moments, fear of losing control, the challenge to my long-held beliefs about life after death. I push them away by weakly pointing to the Qur'an by my bed. My husband acknowledges my request with a nod and picks it up, reading the chapter called Yaseen, knowing it is a particular favorite of mine. I drift away again to the rhythmic sound as the rattling in my chest tells the family surrounding me that I am still hanging on to life. I see beings of light floating by me, the trails of their movement radiant with hues of crystalline reflection. This new world is penetratingly clear to me, sparkling and vibrant, freeing somehow. I see a rippling green meadow in front of me waiting to be crossed. Not yet, I sense, not just yet…

I am brought back to my body abruptly by its silent, insistent, gasping for air. There is a flurry at my bedside as my family tries to soothe me and hold my arms down, caressing them back to my sides. I have long since stopped eating and drinking and have even refused the pain medications. The pain, hopefully purification for my sins of this world, is almost like a separate entity now, greeting me for a few moments before I drift off again…

I am in a different space now, sitting in a huge, red, overstuffed chair. There is a harsh-looking man in the identical chair across and directly in front of me and his smell is of the ages, his pull like a looming black vortex. His provocative voice is telling me that all the doubts I had deep in my heart about Islam were true-that Jesus, the Beautiful One, was truly my Savior and I needed to declare that now before it was too late. I am feeling myself being dragged down into the tempest and I cry out as I did so many times in my life, "Oh God, Oh God, please help me, please save me. Oh God…!" My throat tightens and my hands clench the arms of the chair as I fight the urge to be sucked down. I spit at him – "No, no, he is just a prophet! There is only one god, my God, and Muhammed is His Messenger!" I say it over and over until my voice is a high-pitched wail and the vision disappears, bringing me back to my body – stronger in conviction but much weaker in the mortal sense. I have heard from Shaitan, hopefully for the last time…

THE ANGEL OF DEATH

At length, when death approaches one of you,
Our angels take his soul,
and they never neglect their duty…
[Qur'an, 6: 61]

I AM LYING IN MY BED, but it is in an open space. A majestic creature covered with the accumulation of eons of existence sits by my head. In the distance, as far away as my eyes can see, are two beings of light, fresh and beautiful as the sweetness of faith itself. They are holding a cloth, the color and texture like none I have ever seen. The entity next to my head croons, "Come out, oh you gentle soul, to the pleasure and forgiveness of your Lord." I feel a tug on the inside of my toes and observe my life force begin to move up my legs, light replacing darkness, the gift of Grace replacing bulk. I feel powerless to stop it, but am comforted by the continuous reassuring tone of one I now know to be the Angel of Death. For the 'living' that title has a negative connotation, but his tenderness through this makes me know God is there, watching, guiding, All-Present. As my soul reaches the throat, it moves out of my body like a drop of water from a jug. I lift up, completely free of the bonds of earthly raiment. All fear is gone…

THE FINAL BREATH

Then why do you not intervene
when the soul of the dying man reaches the throat;
and you the while sit looking on?
[Qur'an, 56: 83-84]

MY HUSBAND HAS SQUEEZED MY hand harder, but I can no longer feel it. I had been gasping for air, trying to take in the last bits of this lifetime. My body is agitated, jumpy, more active than it has been in days. With my soul traveling up through my chest, I finally relax, taking a final deep sigh, and with my husband's lips pressed against my forehead, let go of this existence. My husband stands back and looks into the empty caverns that once defined my soul and reaches up to gently pull my eyelids closed.

I am floating above what used to be my body. I am aware of the grief on the faces of my loved ones and want to comfort them and tell them all about the truth of death, but I know that can't happen. I watch my family take turns kissing my pale cheeks and see them struggle with their own mortality…

THE ASCENT

*By those who gently draw out
the souls of the blessed…*
[Qur'an, 79: 2]

AS MY SOUL IS GATHERED up by the pair of glistening beings and deftly wrapped in the beautiful and welcoming cloth they hold open, the fragrance coming from that joyous cloak assails my senses with a mixture of sweet rose water, warming anise and exotic musk. Comfort is too simple a word to convey what I experience. We slowly begin to ascend together, up, up, until we reach the outer rim of the first heaven, the one I glanced longingly up to for most of my time on earth, and as we reach the gate into the second heaven, the angels there gather near us. "Who is this delightful soul?" they ask excitedly. The angels with me call me by my best names from the life, and these questioning angels join us in the climb, and at each of the seven heavens this scenario is repeated, the assemblage and excitement building to a crescendo as my soul is lifted to the final gate at the highest level. As this ornate doorway swings open, I am bathed in light of the most exquisite nature. The angels bow as they hold out their arms and present me to God like a newborn babe. I hear a voice say, "Write the book of My servant in the register of the righteous. Take this soul back down to the earth, because from it I created them, to it I will return them, and from it I will bring them out again."

The descent is swift and will prove to be the last comfort I will feel for a while, for at that moment I am deposited in my grave…

MY SHROUD

"Wherever you are,
Death will find you out,
even if you are in towers
built up strong and high!"
Qur'an, 4: 78]

I AM ABOVE MY BODY, yet still aware and perceiving through its senses. I am lying on a table with a sink at my head, a hose coming out from the side like a thin, black snake. My body has been stripped down except for a cloth over my private parts, and there are two sagacious Muslim women on either side of me, sternly intent on the task ahead. One of them turns to a small table to ready the oil and camphor, and the other positions me for wudu, the ritual cleansing. My hair is rinsed, braided and laid over the edge of the table above me. They begin the washing, gently rocking me, first the right side and then the left, this ritual being repeated three times, the third wash having the camphor added, its lustrous properties lifting me closer to the higher realms. The water feels cool and I can see the angels surrounding us. Surprisingly, my body responds as if it were still alive. The women are quietly making supplication for my forgiveness as they expertly move down my body completing the cleansing bath, and to each plea they make, the angels present say, "Ameen." The angels are also praying for me, and the tidings move from one world to the next effortlessly, everyone working and praying in tandem.

After I am properly washed and dried, my body is oiled, and I am placed on a series of heavy, white cloths. My head is tenderly slipped into an opening in the first cloth, and my chest is then covered with the material. My privates are wrapped diaper-style, and a small skirt is tied onto my midsection and legs. My hair is then covered with a triangular head covering tied in the back, and in the final step, I feel the softness of the cotton cloth as I am completely enfolded in it. I am conscious of the ties being slipped under my body and then fastened around my ankles, legs and chest. I feel a tug as I am lifted up and laid in my coffin, which has been lovingly padded with pillows, evening out the unforgiving slats in the casket for my journey to the grave.

As I am suspended above my body, it is carried into the mosque, the sweetness of well-wishing and pleas for forgiveness lapping against my coffin like waves from the ocean. The religious leader stands at the side of my coffin at waist level, and the prayer of death is prayed for me. The procession to the grave is solemn and quiet, and I note the body that served me so well in this lifetime slowly being lowered into a perfectly chiseled hole in the earth. I feel a gentle thump as my husband jumps into my grave and barely whispers, "Oh love, remember to say the Declaration of Faith; remember the questioning; be strong and firm in your faith. Remember I love you and will, God willing, be with you in the Paradise. He is helped out, and I can hear his footsteps as he reluctantly walks away. I am utterly alone.....

THE GRAVE

From the earth did We create you,
and into it We will return you…
[Qur'an, 20: 55]

THE EFFECT IS INSTANTANEOUS. THE angels swoop down, and I am slammed into my body as they lower me into the grave, and I go from a feeling of effortless being to a barren, desolate, dank existence. The fistfuls of dirt, released in a sequence of three, begin showering down. No isolation on earth could have gotten me ready for this moment of stark aloneness. The truth is that as you age, the body sags downward almost as if the earth is already making its claim on you, but no solitary moment in my living time could compare to the longing I feel now for any companionship. As the blanket of dirt above me is completed, I strain to hear the footsteps as they walk away from my grave. The stillness is deafening as I perceive a slight movement all around me. I am suddenly in the earth's grasp, the soil squeezing me, compressing my body, trying to mingle its essence of clay with mine. I resist, but it is futile, every part of my body feeling the pressure of the crushing caress. Just when I feel I might implode from the sheer force, I sense a lessening, and the dirt retreats to its rightful place. As I lay there reeling from the sudden release, my ears pick up a faint rustling, a swishing sound that seems to grow exponentially within moments. All at once I am sitting up, face to face with a pair of immense creatures with eyes like caldrons and teeth like the horns of a steer. They waste no time, and the one to my left begins, its voice roaring like a thunderstorm, "Who is your Lord?" I shrink from the sound, but find my voice and clearly articulate, "My Lord is Allah!" The other being then shrieks, "What is your religion?" I answer quickly, bolder now. "My religion is Islam!" They both screech in unison, "Who is your prophet?" The pitch is almost unbearable, but I scream back, "My prophet is Muhammed!" They fall silent with my final answer, and I discern the voice of God from above saying, "My servant has told the truth!" Finally these great beings are satisfied, and they rustle away as quickly as they came.

I sense quiet movement around me. I look to my right to see a prayer rug so stunning and ornate it glistens from within. It speaks to me and says, "I am your prayer, and nothing can harm you from this side." I look to the left and see a vessel filled with liquid the color of white silk, and it also speaks, "I am your fasting, and I will protect you from this side." I feel pressure on the top of my head, and as I glance up, a Qur'an with letters of gold proclaims, "You struggled to know me, so I will shield you from above!" I lift my head slightly to see what is unfolding at my feet. My charity, a black velvet drawstring bag with coins pouring out of it like a waterfall, assures me that nothing can reach me from that direction. I then identify the voice of God again instructing the angels to prepare bedding and clothes from Paradise, and my head is turned to the right as a window is opened in my grave to a sight more exquisite than all of earth's beauty combined. My joy gets the better of me then, and I exclaim, "Oh, God! Please let the Day of Judgment start now! I want to see my home and family in the Paradise!" I sigh deeply, contentedly, as the perimeter of my surroundings begins to expand until I can no longer see the edges. A sweet, fresh smell fills my space, and there appears a stunningly beautiful sister wrapped in a garment that seems attached to the skin itself, radiating brilliant colors as she glides along. "Who are you?" I ask delightedly, wondering when the blessings will end. She smiles so warmly I feel the heat penetrating to all the parts of my body that were chilled by the sunless grave. "I am your good deeds and I have come to keep you company until the Day of Standing."

I never thought I would welcome such a wait til now...

THE RESRRECTION

They swear their strongest oath
by Allah that Allah will not
raise up those who die...
[Qur'an, 16: 38]

EVEN WITH THE SPACIOUSNESS OF my grave, there is still a part of me that feels confined, compressed, waiting. The true essence of who I was in the lifetime seems shut away somewhere, peering through…watching for, I don't know, some kind of sign. Most of my physical body has long since dissolved, sorted into the elements of the earth that comprised it. The only fragment left seems to be what I had heard called many times the os sacrum, the Latin words meaning 'sacred bone'; in layman's terms, the tailbone. It is the only connection now to my body and this wonderfully complex receptacle carries the very atoms of who I was on earth. I feel it will be the foundation of my rebirth on the Day the Debts Come Due.

It seems like a millennia since I've been here, visiting my grave to enjoy the beauty and to converse with my 'good deeds' and then going back everyday to the Barzakh or Isthmus for safe keeping. Today is different, however, as there is an intensity in the air - a moisture, if you will. I am gazing out my window to Paradise when I sense a drop of something on me. It tingles as it trickles down; then I am aware of another, and soon, too many drops to differentiate. That compressed, waiting part of me begins to stir. I feel an uncoiling, like a green shoot trying to push through the soil in all four directions, and soon I sense my whole being morphing as the drops from above become a steady stream. What I have been in the grave is receding, and I observe a new form taking shape, one of more substance, more permanence. It is not painful, just expansive. I have new life moving through me, the tendrils from my 'seed' moving up through my limbs and organs, bringing with it something not felt in ages…life!

Just as the unfurling is complete, I have no time to ponder the change as I hear a blaring sound like the blowing of a great horn shaking the very foundation of creation…

ZILZAL

When the earth is shaken
to her utmost convulsion
and the earth throws up
her burdens from within...
[Qur'an, 99: 1-2]

AS THE COVERING OVER MY grave cracks open, my ears are assaulted by the sounds of war. As I am compelled out of my place of repose, I am horrified to see that the war is with the very elements of earth itself. "Oh, God!" I scream, "What's happening to Your creation? Is this the day we were warned about?" I see fissures streaming red in the sky, some parts of the canopy already collapsing and falling to earth. The ocean is a raging inferno, roaring and pitching from the force of the undulating waves as they change from the placid combination of hydrogen and oxygen to the volatile atom of hydrogen alone, trillions of atoms splitting and colliding, dissipating any liquid the ocean contained. The heat is unbearable, and as far as my eye can see there are huge jagged gaps in the terrestrial plane as bodies are being pulled out and thrown down to fend for themselves amid the chaos. Even the surrounding air is being torn down, hanging in strips like worn-out wallpaper. Humanity is now up and witness to a calamity so monstrous, it is unparalled. The cries of, "Oh, what is happening?" and, "Help me, please, help me!" ring in my ears as I dodge the rush of newly formed bodies weaving in and out, no one looking around, just rolling forward to some as yet unnamed goal. The earth as we knew it is crumbling. I am vaguely aware of being naked as I, too, answer the innate call to keep moving. I see people I know everywhere, even my husband, but the misery is so oppressive, there is no recognition. My family is there, in shock and fear, their eyes bulging out and non-blinking, almost as if they had no eyelids. I can't seem to get my bearings. There are so many creatures around me -humans, animals, insects, snakes, melting together now as if from the same wellspring.

I stare in wonder as the steadfast mountains that held our world together crumble to dust, forming tufts as light as air, swirling away with the movement of the crowds. As I find my way through the convulsing fray, I see a change taking place and wonder how this could be. As the contents of the earth go through their transformations, there is a leveling and with each leveling an expansion and with each expansion a linear settling. Incredibly, the earth, as was supposed so many years ago, is becoming flat.

The noise around me has settled down now as we all find our preordained places. There is only mumbling, prayers, and soft moaning. The Day of Reckoning has arrived…

THE DAY OF JUDGMENT

On the Day, We will remove the mountains,
and you will see the earth as a level stretch,
and We will gather them all together,
nor will We leave out any one of them.
[Qur'an, 18: 47]

I FEEL THE SWEAT SLOWLY trickling down my ankles as I glance up to see the sun directly above us, so close I feel I could reach up and touch it. I seem to be one of the blessed ones because as I look around, most people are covered in sweat, some from their knees down, others from their shoulders, and still others gasping, drowning in the very liquid created to keep us cool. The searing, sweltering heat is only one of the many discomforts of this incalculable Day. Although the Day has just begun, it feels like we have been standing in the same spot for a thousand lifetimes. I try to recall my former life on the old earth, but 50 years seems like the blink of an eye. It's as if I spent a day there or part of an afternoon.

Just when I think that I can't take the blistering holocaust one more second, I am lifted up and carried closer to the source of radiating Divine Light, and I start to feel a coolness wash over me as I am deposited under a canopy as alluring and gilded as anything I could have imagined Heaven to be. The effect is immediate, and I am gently laid to rest on a velvety cushion of deep green brocade and gold, assuaging my suffering and bringing me peace. As I sink into the refreshing chill of my new place of repose, my heart at that moment is lifted up, and I am carried to the shore of a river so beautiful it shines like a diamond in the sun. There is a man there whose face is beaming with tender luminosity. His outfit is layered in soft pastels with lines of gold thread running through the folds, each moving as if it wished to caress the wearer. He smiles as if I am a long lost and sorely missed companion. "Assalamulaikum!" he says, as he hands me a cup made of transparent silver so extraordinary that I don't know if the scintillating liquid it contains is the source of light or the vessel itself. I thank him and gratefully drink, and with one sip there is a permanent and abiding end to thirst itself. "What river is this?" I ask in amazement, and he smiles and says, "It is Kawther, the river of Paradise," and that is when I realize that the one human I tried to emulate and love in my living time is standing in front of me, my beloved Prophet! I am home…

I peer out of my canopy onto the rest of humanity and thank God once again for His mercy. I keep running one certain verse of the Qur'an through my mind over and over, "Did you then think We created you in jest and you would not be brought back?"

The moaning and sobbing goes in waves, sometimes reaching an ear-piercing crescendo and then receding like the great breakers of an ocean. I see eyes staring fixedly in horror, everyone grouped together behind their respective leaders, some behind the politicians they followed, other behind the celebrities they adored, and others behind the prominent leaders of gods falsely worshipped. There is a constant agitation moving through their sweat-stained bodies and no comfort to be found for them anywhere. They are left to the memories of all that they perpetrated on the earth, making them bite their hands in anguish, heedless of the pain, aware of the truth around them.

I watch from my oasis as a group of frustrated souls get together and run from prophet to prophet, begging for them to intercede with God for the Judgment to begin, but they are told to go to the next prophet and the next... Finally they come to Prophet Muhammed, the best of mankind, and his beatific gaze settles on them, bringing them a treasured moment of peace. "Oh Muhammad, Oh Praised One, won't you please call on your Lord to begin the Reckoning? We don't even care about the outcome; we can no longer tolerate this scorching trial!" As he stands to his full height, his eyes fill with tender, sorrowful emotion. "Yes," he replies, "I am the only messenger who did not use the supplication God granted us in the lifetime, and I will use it now!" As quick as lightning, he runs to The Magnificent on His throne and throws himself down into prostration, begging for the Reckoning to start. We hear words of adoration never before spoken by man come from his tongue as Al Wahhab, The Granter of all things, gives him the permission.

The clamor of the multitudes is hushed by the presence of their Lord, The Ultimate Judge...

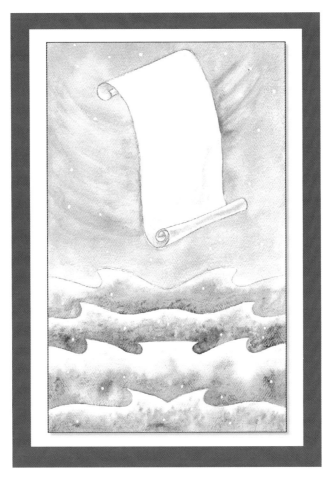

FACING ALLAH

Then he that will be given his Book of Deeds
in his right hand will say, "Ah, here!
Read my Record. I did really think
that my account would one day reach me!"
[Qur'an, 69: 19-20]

THE TIME IS HERE. BLINDING panic has caught the murmurs of speculation in humanity's throat. We hear a deafening whoosh of air above us and then what sounds like a thunderous waterfall, and as our heads snap to look up, billions and billions of books are descending on us. We instinctively know what is coming, and some of those waiting are in such terror that every hair on their head turns white in an instant. I stand with my right arm stretched up, hoping, praying, anticipating… After a tortuous interlude, I finally feel a distinctive 'slap' as my Book of Deeds lands squarely in my right hand. The relief washes over me as I clutch it to my chest, weeping for joy and crying, "Oh, God, oh, God…" over and over again.

We shuffle past our Lord in ranks as we position for the roll call of names. Those of us who can submit in prostration do so, but many don't seem to have the ability to bend. They try to bow rigidly, but even that is denied them. I can only think that prostration was not a habit for them in their lifetimes, so it is taken away now.

As the names begin to be called, ripples of shame move through the crowd as we hear the sins of each individual soul announced by God, and then the regretful reply is made. We shudder as we realize that not a mustard seed of good or evil is left out. We hear the many questions - is your prayer complete; is your fasting complete; your life and how did you use it; your knowledge and did you practice it; your money, how did you gain it, and how did you spend it; your body, how did you use it; your spare time; your covenants; your sight; your hearing; your mind…the list goes on and on, and we scramble to find the answers that will please our Lord when our turn comes. This process makes us feel more exposed than standing in our bare skin ever could. The mortifying videos of moral weakness intensify our own personal agony, and we dig even deeper to recall all we may have done. My only respite from this living nightmare comes from remembering a prophetic line I heard in the lifetime, "God will not combine two moments of fear together. If you feared Him in the lifetime, you will have no fear on the Day of Reckoning."

I cling to that thought as something near me catches my eye. I take a moment from reflection to notice that everyone in my group is glowing with white light. Their feet, hands, and faces shine like the markings on a thoroughbred horse, and I glance down to notice that I, too, am glowing with them. "Ah, I muse, the mark of the ritual cleansing before prayer!" I relax ever so slightly with that and marvel that such a small thing could be so very significant now.

My relaxation is short-lived as I hear my named called by the angels. My heart seizes up as I am drawn forward and am enveloped in a noble, shimmering aura so sweet it makes me forget any bad that ever happened to me. I am swept along by the desire to find the source of this warmth and never to depart from it. I feel like I am facing a mammoth typhoon in a row boat as I hear a resounding voice saying, "Oh, My slave, are you ready to acknowledge the blessings I bestowed on you in the life-time?" I am suspended in light, but hear myself say, "Yes, my Lord!"

Then comes the dreaded list, every sin, every mistake, every slander, every word taken in vain, every broken vow, every hurt I ever caused rolled out as if on an ethereal scroll. This comprehensive video begins at the moment I made the Declaration of Faith, and ends when my soul reaches the throat. I regretfully acknowledge each and every wrong of the painful litany until I believe I am doomed to the fire. My anguish reaches heights I never thought possible. To think that I would not be allowed to be close to my Lord is more than I can bear, and my defeat seems imminent…

THE SCALE – WEIGHING OF THE DEEDS

*Then he whose balance of good deeds will be found heavy
will be in a life of good pleasure and satisfaction,
but he whose balance of good deeds will be found light
will have his home in a pit of blazing fire.*
[Qur'an, 101: 6-9]

AS WE LOOK TO OUR Lord for His final judgment, I raggedly reflect on part three of this, our final exam. Part one was the oral exam, seeing if we knew the truth and acquired the knowledge that went with it by answering probing questions about our money, health and time on the Day of Standing. Part two, the written exam, came with our Book of Deeds, opened to see if we understood the truth by our actions on earth. This, then, was part three, the practical, what intentions and actions brought us to this decisive moment where our deeds could either bring us to the Paradise or the Hellfire.

I am brought out of my soul-searching revelry by the sight of a great golden scale appearing in front of the throng, its massive disks on either side hanging from sturdy gold chains suspended on slender rods of textured silver. The pure light and sweet smell of the disk on the right tells us that side will weigh our good deeds. The murmurs get louder now, mingled with sobbing and deep sighs of regret. There is a sound mixed in that is not of human origin, and our personal torment is so great we don't heed its cry until it is almost upon us. We are finally able to discern an unmistakable crackling, and the roaring and pitching are brazen now as millions of angels come into view, harnessed in black iron bridles, straining with all of their might to move their burden forward. We begin to feel warmth that quickly turns to a torrid heat as our eyes stare at the object of their toil. As they slowly move nearer, there are sparks as big as houses flying in every direction, and a fetid stench fills the air. A rolling inferno, gasping, chomping, churning on itself as it reaches out to grasp onto more…its hunger for fuel to keep the unrestrained flame alight has become unquenchable. The howl of the damned has reached fever pitch as their eyes roll back in their heads. They know they have just caught a glimpse of their hideous new abode, and their quaking bodies seem ready to burst apart. The iron-swathed angels drag their beast left to a spot beside the scale, and the flames lick the disk on the left in anticipation, as if already tasting their victims.

As I and my companions around me watch the scene unfold, we are protected from the heat by a veil of light. Our attention is drawn to our right as the soothing sound of birds singing and leaves rustling in a cooling breeze begin to challenge the Hellfire for recognition. There is an audible gasp as we are gifted with the sight of brilliant greens, sensuously ripened fruits and crisp blue rivers, all these elements of heavenly delight exuding a luster enhanced by the Divine Light pouring into them from all sides. When we are finally able to breathe again, the hope in our good deeds and God's Mercy becomes even more fervently wished for. My comfort at that moment comes from one of my favorite teachings, where our Prophet says that when God created Mercy, He separated it into a hundred parts. He gave the earth and everything in it one part only; all the mercy and tenderness you see around you, mother and child, the innate caring in the animal kingdom comes from just this part. He kept the other ninety-nine parts for this, The Day of Judgment. All Praise is due to Him!

We watch, hope mixed with unease, as the weighing begins. Some souls have all their deeds piled on the left and nothing on the right and you can see the realization of remorse etched into their faces. Some are balanced equally with good and bad, and you see a flow of tiny specks no bigger than mustard seeds come flying towards the disk on the right, and soon these 'seeds' of goodness tip the scales to the good. That person rejoices unabashedly as relief washes over him.

One man's weighing has us all riveted, as corruption after deceit is piled on the left disk until it's a veritable mountain of bad deeds, a dark and writhing mass of evil choices over his lifetime, and nothing is on the right, not even a sliver of good. He stands next to his deeds, his eyes staring, streaming with tears and his heart so high in his throat that he can't speak. The high-pitched sounds of an animal in distress come pouring out as he steals a glance at the blistering mass to his left, bellowing with delight at the thought of being fed. All at once God drops a tiny scroll on the disk to his right, and every single one of his deeds is catapulted into the air, and dissipates like fireworks on a starry night. He runs to the disk and opens the scroll to find something written in perfect calligraphy. His lips move slowly as he mumbles the Kalimah, "La illaha Ill Allah, There is no god but God." He bows his head to his Lord and kisses the scrap of paper that saved him from eternal damnation. I watch in amazement as this happens over and over again, and I think, "The glory of God that this tiny slip of paper could outweigh a lifetime of bad deeds.

My turn finally comes, and I see my bad choices being piled on the left. It thankfully is only a small hill, and I wait anxiously as my good deeds start to grow on the right, first balancing the scale, and then as more and more are put on, the scale begins to lean to the right, and then good deeds come from everywhere and land softly on the pile until I realize that there is no way I could have done that much good in my short time on earth. I watch as my bad deeds, too, are sent spiraling skyward. I say, "Oh God, I know these were not my good deeds," and the answer comes, "Yes, my slave, but every good deed you did resulted in another carrying the deed on to another, which adds to your reward without decreasing any reward given to your followers." I am then gathered to my Lord to hear the words that are like cooling salve on an open wound, "Oh, my obedient slave, I covered you in the lifetime, and I forgive you now!" The ecstasy of that moment will live forever in my memory.

I am pleased that I 'studied' for my finals…

SIRAT AL MUSTAQEEM

Not one of you but will pass over it;
this is, with your Lord,
a decree that must be accomplished…
[Qur'an, 19: 71]

WE ARE SENT DOWN A pathway, and as we move forward we begin to discern a stench indescribable. We can't see anything yet, but the sounds are unmistakable – a cacophony of wretchedness, the scream of tortured souls barely audible above the crackling and roaring of a raging fire. It takes a very long time to get close enough to understand, but as the scene unfolds our hearts sink.

We see a cavernous pit over which is suspended a blade as thin as a hair. The pit, recognizable now as the source of the stench, contains the blazing bodies of those unfortunate ones who didn't have enough light to carry them over the Sirat al Mustaqeem, the bridge over Hell. As we watch and wait for our turn over the seething caldron, we see beings so filled and surrounded with light that they fly over the blade. Some have enough light to run quickly, and some have only enough to slowly limp, stopping when it goes dark on the path to wait for their few good deeds to light their way to the end. They must keep moving to avoid the grasp of the hooks of the Fire along the side of the trail. There are many we see that have little or no light at all and they are hooked by these claw-like appendages and thrown into the churning chasm of writhing humanity and demons. Even from far away, the heat is searing our faces, and this is the moment that I wish I had spent all my time in good deeds. The TV shows, movies, idle talk and useless lifetime pursuits haunt me with a deep regret. I pray that I have enough light for a fleeting journey over this abyss of smoking flesh. I am very close now…

As my turn comes, I step gingerly onto the blade and feel lightness in my step. I seem to have perfect balance as I am lifted forward, the light moving in front of me, dancing along, showing the next step and the next. All around me are gleaming hooks, snapping, pursuing, and dragging down bodies, the screams of the lost souls mingling with the unfortunates who have already been snatched by the insatiable fire. My way seems sure though, and I quickly see the end of the Sirat, pure white and beckoning. I take my final step over the pit and wade into rippling green grass, fragrant with the smell of camphor and musk. Each step taken fills me with a cautious hope…

THE BRIDGE OF QISAS

*And to every soul will be paid
in full the fruit of its deeds, and
Allah knows best all that they do.*
[Qur'an, 39: 70]

43

WE SEEM TO BE IN the early evening of this interminable day, the Day of Account, and are being herded towards a bridge, compelling by its balanced nature. As we get nearer, I see people standing in pairs facing one another. Some are slapping the face of their partner, with the receiver merely accepting; some are giving back bits of material; others are receiving what looks like gold; others are pleading tearfully, trying to apologize as they cup their partners' faces tenderly in their hands. As they mete out God's perfect justice, I remember our Prophet saying that Paradise is pure and will only accept that which is pure, and suddenly all of this comes clear. As they finish their tasks, the people quietly move over the bridge to another staging area underneath. In the vast open field surrounding the bridge, there are beasts of every kind pairing off to give or receive their justice. There are horned goats being gored by those without horns, lions being chased and brought down by swift gazelles, rabbits swallowing snakes alive, and sparrows with huge talons clutching screaming hawks as they try to escape their captors. As each of the beasts gets his injustices reckoned, a balancing takes place and he immediately turns into dust and is no more. The humans, who during their lifetimes refused to believe, watch this longingly from their places in the Fire, realizing now they won't be this fortunate.

As I step onto the bridge, I am immediately met by a long line of people I had wronged in my time on earth, and I try with as much love and caring as I can to make things right. It is a painful and heart-wrenching process that I see now would have been so much easier to fix with a kind word of contrition at the time of transgression. I spend my time apologizing for the backbiting and broken vows, as the faces of everyone I ever hurt move past me in procession. I, too, am paraded past other souls who wish to render justice, and I am tortured by the hurt and pain I caused. Oh, how I wish the lifetime would have found me holding my tongue…

As we move along, our hearts become lighter and lighter with each justice recompensed. As the last soul crosses the bridge, a transformation takes place in us that is both cleansing and purifying. Our bodies seem to be expanding, filling with a serene radiance, morphing and taking on a new form, one of towering height, unending youth, and beauty unparalleled. We move along the fragrant meadow toward the source of an emanating brilliance…rushing toward the reward of our life of striving…

PARADISE

*...For the righteous are Gardens
in nearness to their Lord
with rivers flowing beneath:
therein is their eternal home,
with spouses purified and the
good pleasure of Allah...*
[Qur'an, 3: 15]

I LOOK UP FROM THE fragrant meadow and see Paradise with its tall gates open wide, luminescent and beckoning. I have finally arrived at the doorway of my true ancestral home, the home of my parents, Adam and Eve. Ah…Paradise! The angels surrounding the gates are calling out to us excitedly, "Salam, Salam, Salam, Peace, Peace, Peace," inviting us to come through their doorway, praising us for the life we led that brought us to them. We rush forward in anticipation as some of us are called from Riyan, the fasting gate; others are called from the gate of jihad or striving, and still others are called from the gate of charity. Some are being called by all eight of the entry ways and have a delicious choice to make. As we gather at the appropriate gateways, the mood is electric. There is no pushing or shoving; we are so grateful to be there that all traces of impatience or anger with our brothers and sisters are gone, vanished, never to return. All we can do is repeat the cry of the angels, "Salam, Salam, Salam," as we slowly move through the welcoming gates and into the compound.

It is there that we realize the truth of the prophetic saying, "Paradise is what no eye has ever seen, no ear has ever heard, and no heart has ever imagined." It is as if the earthly world were completely devoid of any color or beauty at all, as I feel myself going from desolate and unadorned to sheer abundance. My eyes are taken from a lifetime of sepia tones to brilliant, full-spectrum color so vivid I feel like my eyes are splashed with its hues. I feel myself changing from a flat and transparent entity to a multidimensional being with facets like a diamond, each façade pulling in its own distinct sensation from the immeasurably luxuriant surroundings.

We are approached by joyful young men with gloriously radiant skin, and they hand us tiny golden plates filled with an appetizer so exquisite that if it were all we had for eternity, it would satisfy. We no sooner finish this delicacy and we are given glistening goblets filled to the brim with a silky, tantalizing fluid that moves through our bodies, washing away any traces of thirst endured on The Day of Inevitable Truth now behind us.

As our faces beam with contentment, the next course put before us for our pleasure is ox meat so tender and juicy it erases all memory of anything eaten before this. We remark on the sumptuous flavor of musk, and deduce that the beast must have grazed freely on the grass of this Blessed land.

When we have eaten and drunk our fill, we start drifting away, moving towards the many levels of our homes in this Promised Land. No one has to tell us where to go; we know our addresses better than we knew our homes in the lifetime. As I move through the crowd, eager for a glimpse of my abode here, I am suddenly lifted up and carried to the level above, and I ask the angels what is happening. They inform me that my husband's suffering in the lifetime raised him to a higher rank than me, and that I was being taken to his level. As we glide forward, the angels stop at an elegant tree with a golden trunk and gold branches hanging heavy with fruit, the measure of which is fifty times any earthly fruit. They point to a particularly stunning, pear-shaped fruit, and it splits open to reveal a shimmering mother-of-pearl gown with matching scarf and sandals. They gather this up, and we continue on until we come to a palace so exotic and exquisite it is difficult for me to extol its praises. I say, "Oh, no. This can't be ours! It's too beautiful," but to my joy and amazement they confirm that it is. I look again and marvel at the gold and silver brick design that defies any earthly architectural genius.

We move through the front door, more of a glowing portal, into a space so pleasing to the eye that I just know it was decorated by the angels. There are green brocade couches and pillows lovingly contoured to fit our new bodies, and the graceful colors chosen only add to the room's perfection. Nothing stops the flow of the eye as I turn around and around trying to take in the harmony of it all. The angels smile as they gently prod me to hurry and change into my gown and get ready to greet my husband at the door. The clothes swirl around and mold to my body like a second skin, and the scarf wraps itself through my hair adeptly as it frames my face with a soft blue light. I look and feel radiant as I stand at the doorway in loving anticipation…

I finally catch a glimpse of my husband as he meanders through the plants and bushes on his land. He so desperately wanted property in the lifetime, but the look on his face tells me he is overwhelmingly glad that he waited patiently for his real estate here. His body has taken the shape of all the dwellers of Paradise. He has peerless height, the rarest of beauty, and a vibrant ageless appeal. I thank God again for giving him peace, as I see him catch a glimpse of his new home and watch his mouth drop open in amazement. He scans the perimeter brick by brick until eventually his gaze rests on the glow of the woman in the doorway. The delight and awe I see in his eyes makes up for any deficiencies I felt I had in our earthly life. He stops abruptly in his tracks, unable or unwilling to move, just staring in appreciation at this vision of his partner. We stay like that in mutual love and wonderment for what seems like years. It is difficult to know how long because time means nothing within infinity. We are finding out that the perfection of forever is that you can do what you want for as long as you want and go where you want anytime you want.

I finally break the spell and wave him in, and he awakens out of his standing dream and greets me with "Assalamulaikum, Peace be upon you, my beautiful wife!" I pull him into our home, and we walk around looking at everything, giving thanks to God at every stop. Our servants bring us indescribable fare as we eat and drink to our heart's content. They then suggest that we take a tour of the grounds, and we tear ourselves away from our palace and start walking.

We don't get very far when we begin to hear the rushing of water. In an instant we are beside a crystalline river flowing between the banks of musky sand. Our guide dips a silver cup in the liquid and gives us the first taste of our river in Paradise. The satiny liquid delights the amplified senses we were gifted with when we entered the Garden, and as we drink cup after cup our guide informs us that we have three more rivers to visit on our property, one of honey, one of milk, and the other of wine and that each one is better than the last. We hurry along to their rolling banks, and as we move through our rivulets one by one, we remark each time that, "Nothing could be better than this!" and at each one, we find something better. We find milk so white it gleams as it cascades down the slope, honey so pure it defies description, and a wine that gives clarity not confusion. All we can do on our sojourn of streams is repeat, "Subhan Allah, Subhan Allah, Subhan Allah, the Glory of God," as each experience brings us more ecstasy than the last. As we languish under the shade of one of our many giant trees, the shade given by leaves as large as elephant ears, we still can't find words to describe what we are seeing. The most wondrous gardens of earth look like dry stubble next to this plethora of exotic plants and trees. Everything about it fills the senses with pleasure and well-being. The purity of mood is enhanced by the Divine Light diffused through every inch of our surroundings, and we are lifted to new heights, yet again, as we remember for a brief moment where we could have been if not for the Grace of God. Part of our setting here is looking through the windows given to us into the Hellfire. We watch, with a mixture of relief and pity, those who are being punished in the harshest way, and we are grateful to have been chosen to be of the dwellers of Paradise.

We hear someone calling for us to come to the market at the center of town, and as we arrive, we realize that all of the inhabitants of this land must be here. The residents of the Fire are also gathered, and as we stare at them through the windows, a huge ram with great curved horns is brought forth for all to see. We are told that this ram represents death, and to our delight and the horror of the dwellers of Hell, the beast is slaughtered before our eyes, and we are told that this marks the end of Death in any form. Joy is bursting out from inside of us as we realize the beauty and pleasure of Paradise is ours forever. We hear the moaning of the damned as they, too, are struck with this realization of the end of Death, but our attention is quickly drawn to the Throne of our Lord. With faces as bright as the brightest stars, we all turn to face Him. Just when we think we will explode with happiness, our Incomparable and Majestic Lord removes the veil from in front of Him and our rapture is absolute. We are at the pinnacle of contentment, and bliss fills every corner of our being.

This is what we were striving for in our earthly lives…this perfect, harmonic moment of knowing the total pleasure of Allah…we are complete…

HELLFIRE
Fate of a Sealed Heart

ILLNESS BEFORE DEATH

...Those whose efforts have been wasted
in this life while they thought that
they were acquiring good by their works...
[Qur'an, 18: 104]

AS I LAY HERE BARELY able to move my limbs, I feel trapped. I can do nothing but think, running my brief life over and over in my head. I know that death is close now, and I try to gather my beliefs. I attempted to live a good life and to be kind to people. I didn't cheat, lie, steal, or murder and I tried not to hurt anyone if I could help it. I struggled through as best I could and had everything a human strives for to live a good life. I had an adoring family, a sizeable house, beautiful cars, lots of good food, and so many wonderful vacations that I can't count them. I feel like I can leave this world now and finally rest, letting my body slowly turn to dust. Ah, to feel no more pain or sorrow, just tranquil nothingness. I never believed in life after death, and I can't see any reason to start now. These beliefs I hold were good enough for my parents and their parents, and I believe I am just another inhabitant of this planet whose time has come. Surrounded by my loving family, I stoically await that time. Finally, to the wails and moans of my relatives I shudder, getting ready to breathe my last…

ANGEL OF DEATH

*If you could see when the angels take
the souls of the unbelievers at death,
how they smite their faces and their backs, saying,
"Taste the chastisement of the Blazing Fire..."*

[Qur'an, 8: 50]

I CAN FEEL MYSELF FADING away…I look forward to the end, when I will finally be at peace. Things are getting blacker and blacker until…wait, what is this? I suddenly find my eyes wide open looking onto a new severe reality laid out in front of me, like my life was a dream and this is my real time. I flash on what a newborn must feel like as it gets its first glimpse of life outside the womb. I am on an open plain, and an immense, brooding man-like creature with jet black hair and clothing and a smell gathered from the worst of the earth is at my head. I am terrified to see a blaze of fire and smoke coming from his nose and mouth, and he immediately begins bellowing at me, "Come out to the anger and wrath of your Lord!" I see far off in the distance two beings with sinister-looking clothing and tar-streaked faces, and they are holding a cloth that seems to pulsate with a venomous glare, as if it has been smoldering in a vile place for centuries. All around us is a stench so foul I would give anything to be far away from it. "Oh, what is this? Who are these monsters? What's happening to me?" I am screaming now, trying to get away from them as my life force is being ripped out of my toes, the sensation moving up my legs as I squirm to get free. A torrid, searing heat is closing in on me as I feel my soul start to run around in my body, trying to avoid the creature's grip. I am besieged now as more angry beings show up and start beating my back and face, screaming, "Taste the burning of the fire. This is because of your deeds! God is never unjust to His servants!" I am pummeled over and over as my soul is unwillingly pulled to my throat, each movement causing excruciating pain, as if I'm being torn limb from limb. I can see this dark, looming entity looking at my grieving family with a sharp gaze. His voice is a hushed whisper as he says, "Cry for yourselves … I'll be coming back again and again…"

THE FINAL BREATH

Then why do you not,
if you are exempt from future account,
call back the soul if you are true
in your claim of independence?
[Qur'an, 56: 86-87]

MY FAMILY SURROUNDS THE BED as I lay gasping for breath. They stroke my hair and arms as I finally give up trying to hold onto the air no longer willing to sustain me. My body goes limp as I open my eyes for one last glimpse of the world I so treasured. My loved ones move closer now, realizing the end is near. There is silence, my final breath leaving slowly, reluctantly, relishing each stratum as it exits the lungs. It moves quickly through the throat, languishing in the mouth for a moment before finally being pushed past my lips. Those around me wait for what seems like an eternity for my inhale, but it never comes, and the moaning and wailing begin as the moment of my demise hits them. There are choruses of, "She is in a much better place now," and "She will finally have some peace." Everyone nods at that as the tears flow freely. Someone gently reaches over to close my eyes as my lifeless body slumps further into the stiff white sheets. The grieving turns to soft whispers as the living quietly turn away to leave…

The scene is total chaos as my soul is peeled out of my body like wet wool from a thorny branch, the tearing of tendons and the cracking of bones only audible on this side of the veil of life. The enraged being at my head holds my essence for less than an instant before I am handed to the tar-faced beings, who quickly wrap my beleaguered soul in a cloth so rough I feel the prink of a thousand needles. The heat of this stifling cloak begins scalding my skin almost immediately, and the stench is unbearable…Please! PLEASE!! Is there no one to help me?

THE ASCENT

*To those who reject Our signs and treat them with arrogance,
no opening will there be of the gates of Heaven, nor will
they enter the Garden until the camel can pass through
the eye of the needle: such is Our reward for those in sin...*
[Qur'an, 7: 40]

THINGS ARE MOVING SO QUICKLY I can't process what's happening. Who are these beings, and where are they taking me? The reeking, foul smell of this grating garment is choking me, and the incessant heat is making my brain boil. I feel a jerk upwards as my dark companions on either side of me begin an ascent. Up, up, we go until we reach a gate of sorts and more of these light beings gathered there. I hear the disgust in their voices as they exclaim, "Who is this evil soul?" My captives tell them I am so and so, with me recognizing some of the worst names I was called in my lifetime. How did they know? They seem to know everything about me, while I am only able to guess who they are. I am jostled around until I am lifted up to the gatekeepers, and just being close to the gate brings some much needed peace. The light around the gate is tranquil and compelling, and my soul hopes against hope that this is my final resting place and that this nightmare might finally come to an end. I am brought in front of the doors and the beings ask for them to be opened, and yes, I want to enter there, more than I ever wanted anything before, but the doors remain closed to me. Sadness overwhelms me as I behold an angry voice boom, "Throw this unbelieving soul back down to the earth to be punished for her disobedience!"

I am experiencing a tortuous and swift descent to my grave as I am slammed into this dark, smelly, cold, and unwelcoming hole in the ground. The feeling is of desolation as I am ripped away from the only source of true peace I have ever felt, and I am devastated by an inner knowledge that my soul will never be warmed by that light again…

MY SHROUD

*Often will those who disbelieve wish
that they had been Muslims.
Leave them alone to eat and enjoy,
and let false hope distract them:
for soon they will know...*
[Qur'an, 15: 2-3]

THE ASSAULT ON MY SOUL as I am suspended over my body is relentless. The anguished howls of my tortured spirit echo through the stark hospital halls, filling the place of my demise. I realize now that human ears cannot hear my screams or come to my aid. As I peer down at my body, the attendants are cleaning my once vibrant skin and speaking in hushed tones as they expertly lift me and place me in the body bag. The scene is the antithesis of the battering and recriminations going on above it, and as my earthly envelope is wheeled down the hall and out the back door to the gleaming black hearse, I follow it, trying to get away from the scourge of these messengers of foreboding. Everywhere I turn there is a new pain to endure, a new accusation I must own up to. As I make the aerial journey down the street, I long to be back in that body, away from this onslaught.

The punishment continues through the many hours it takes to embalm my body at the funeral home. As my blood and fluids are drained, they are replaced with an acrid substance designed to preserve my body for a little longer, but it only makes my body more ghastly and unnatural. I observe as they glue my eyes shut, making sure I never gaze upon this beautiful earth again, and I wince as a wire is shot through my chin to keep my mouth closed, creating a final silence. My hair is neatly arranged around my face…only the front needs doing as I will be lying down soon. I recognize the dress I wore many times to all the gay and festive affairs, and as strangers pull it on my lifeless body, I feel a longing to have my life back the way it was. As I witness, my body is laid in the coffin with the top half open so my friends and relatives can see me and touch me one more time. I look puffy and unreal as the curtains are opened to a crowd of the bereaved. Fresh tears flow as they file past my corpse, sometimes putting a hand on my cold skin, sometimes stopping to pray, and sometimes whispering words they wanted to say to me when

I was alive, but didn't have the strength or courage to say. I am hovering above all the grieving and mourning in a much greater quandary than death. As I am beaten over and over again by the beings around me, the ache of regret is sinking in. The truth hangs heavy through the bitter pain as I realize I will pay dearly for my lack of belief in My Creator and the Hereafter. I dart amongst my living relatives, begging them to help me and save me from this truth, but they are heedless of my imploring. As the casket is closed, I feel finality to the life I lived and a deep yearning to be back. I follow the procession to the graveyard with my company of grim, tormenting companions in tow. "Maybe once I am laid in the grave this battering will be over," I earnestly hope, but a voice deep inside me knows it won't happen that way.

As my body is lowered into the ground, I feel my soul being pulled towards the cold, barren figure. I go with this pull, wondering what grueling trials await…

THE GRAVE

*Whatever misfortune happens to you
is because of the things
your hands have wrought...*
[Qur'an, 42: 30]

THE MEETING OF BODY AND soul in this underground ren-
dezvous is harsh and unadorned. I feel trapped, constricted, and it's so
pitch dark I feel like I'm blind. My sense of hearing is acute, and the echo
of footsteps receding confirms my aloneness. This is not at all what I
thought death would be. I thought at worst, I would just go to sleep forever, and at best, I would be with my long-dead relatives somewhere.
Never did I expect the kind of interaction with determined beings of
light, or refusals at celestial gates, and surely not the sheer cold and closing darkness I am aware of now. As I lie trying to gather my thoughts, I
feel a shift around me, a loss of breath, as the earth squeezes me in a death
grip. I hear the grave hiss, "No welcome for you today. You were the
worst of creatures that walked on my back. Now you are here and will
see my work!"

"Oh! Please stop," I scream, as my ribs are crushed together by the
force of the pressure. The pain is excruciating as my chest implodes, and
I howl as the grip of the earth becomes tighter and tighter, until I feel like
I'm being pushed through a keyhole. Just when I feel that I'm carrying
the weight of the earth and everything in it, the sensation begins to sub-
side, and the rolling dirt expands and pulls back away from me. I barely
have time to breathe when I am besieged by two creatures larger and more
horrifying than the one at my death. They have eyes like blackened pots
and teeth like great horned rams, and they close in on me from both sides.
The one on the left screeches at me, "Who is your Lord?" I stutter as I
try to think of an answer that will satisfy him. "Huh? What? I don't
know!" I squirm to get away from them, but they persist. The one on
the right bellows, "What is your religion?" Again I search for the words to
quiet them. I lived only for the lifetime. My religion was of fun and self-
satisfaction. I didn't believe there was anything more. I knew religious
people, but I thought they were wasting their lives by denying themselves

what life had to offer. I thought it crazy to put that much effort into something so 'intangible'. I am beginning to realize the depth of my mistakes and regret is not far behind. Now my stammering is proof of my ignorance, and I spit out, "Umm, I'm not sure!" I feel a sense of rage building in my interrogators as the third question comes at me. "Who is your Prophet?" Now I know I am lost. I followed movie stars, sports stars, the wealthy, and the powerful of the earth, blindly unaware of any goodness the prophets brought, and now it has come back to haunt me. I can't even manage a grunt to this one, and I give up in morose resignation as a gleaming sledgehammer is raised above my head, and I am struck only once, my body shattering to pieces, experiencing the height of pain this present form can feel. It is at this moment that I recognize the same voice I heard at the gate, only this time it is filled with seething wrath as it says, "My slave is a liar! Make her a grave from Hellfire, and furnish it from Hellfire, and open a window to Hellfire!" I turn my head to the left and see a scene so frightening and gruesome that it is as if I never felt any good in my lifetime. My only reality now is this churning, smoking inferno called Hell. That word seldom crossed my lips in the lifetime, except to curse, but now I worry it will be my reality forever. My self-loathing is brought to a crescendo when a second window opens next to the first, and it starkly contrasts with serenity, beauty, fruits, rivers, and white light that can only be described as the Divine pulsating through everything. I keep looking from one window to the other as I hear a voice say, "This is where you could have been had you believed!" I sob with remorse, but feel deep inside of me the truth of this moment, the bare reality of what is in front of me.

My grave seems to get darker and shrinks even more so that my arms can hardly stay at my sides. The blackness suddenly fills with the stench of rotting flesh as a hideous female shape wrapped in filthy old clothing comes into view. "Oh! No! Who are you?" I ask, as my senses reel. "I am your bad deeds, and I will be keeping you company until the Day of Judgment," she yelps gleefully. That is the moment that I completely lose it. "Please, let me out, let me go back to the lifetime! I will live the way you want me to; I will believe in what you tell me to; I will do good deeds, give to the poor, anything you ask! Is there any way out now?" I am screaming, a deep primal sound, piercing in its desperation. The voice gruffly says, "No! Taste the punishment you swore would never come to you! Taste the fruits of your arrogance!" I become quiet then, great wracking sobs moving through me as the truth sinks in. I hunker down in complete and utter wretchedness, feeling the bars of my prison around me. The hammer is being raised, and as I am smashed to dust over and over again, great reptilian creatures breathing fire come into my space, scratching and biting me everywhere. They are flinging my bad deeds at me as they tear at my flesh, and I am savagely told they will do this until the Day of Reckoning. As I stare at the window of fire, I wonder when respite will come…

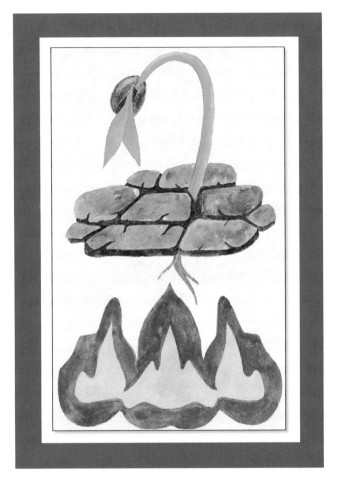

THE RESURRECTION

*...and they sometimes say:
There is nothing except our life
on this earth, and never shall
we be raised up again..."*
[Qur'an, 6: 29]

THE SAMENESS IS MADDENING. EVERYDAY I am dragged from the isthmus or keeping place to my grave to face the tearing of flesh and the battering of the hammer. As I approach the pit that is my distasteful refuge, the stench is overpowering. That grotesque figure is always there reminding me of my lifetime of ignorance on earth, and there is no light and no peace and certainly no rest. I remember the saying we spewed out so casually in the living time, "No rest for the wicked," and this is playing itself out here. I am forced to view the two contrasting windows in my grave with deep and growing regret. I feel the heat of the fire and taste the poisonous pus that will be my sustenance there. I see where I am headed on account of my arrogance and disbelief and regrettably, I see where I could have been if I had only heeded the call. The contrast is like tranquil light and foreboding darkness, searing heat and gentle shade, joy and utter debasement. Any Divine Light gifted to me in the lifetime has been extinguished, and I am filled with despair. The year upon year spent in this hellish fissure have seen my body dissolve into the darker elements of the earth, leaving only a portion of my previous body, my tailbone, holding the very seeds of my existence. This part seems to be waiting…watching…petrified with fear…

This day, though, the usually stale air feels different-not lighter, but something has shifted. I sense the sound of liquid hitting the dirt around me and begin to perceive the drops on my form. The tingling caused by their contact feels like a bit of respite, and I pray that my torment has come to an end. As I am covered with this liquid, I feel a stirring…an expanding…an awakening of the essence of me that never left. Oh, if only this change would get me away from the tumult of this place, I would never ask for another thing. I begin to shoot up and out in all four directions now, and new life seems to course through my veins. I feel the transformation almost complete now, but I am filled with trepidation as my newly formed ears hear a sound so thunderous it cracks the covering above me, and for a split second I breathe in fresh air. "Finally," I sigh, "Relief!" I look up, my heart daring to entertain a ray of hope…

ZILZAL

Oh mankind! Fear your Lord!
For the convulsion of
the Hour of Judgment
will be a thing terrible…
[Qur'an, 22: 1]

THE BREATH OF FRESH AIR I took in is almost knocked out of me as two beings grab me and propel me up and out of my chasm of horror to an event that dwarfs any pain or suffering I may have felt for these millennia. My naked body is cast down on its face, and as I raise my head I see unspeakable chaos and destruction. The sky has cracked…CRACKED! The canopy we took for granted is falling down in huge chunks. The earth is convulsing, and filthy debris, the waste of eons of human consumption and greed, is snaking out of her like lava from an erupting volcano. I look in the distance and see a churning, crackling ocean dissipating as its elements collide and release their metabolic energy to the space that was once our air. The mountains are becoming shifting sands, dust really, getting blown around by the drunken movements of humanity awakened. The crush of newly formed bodies is suffocating as they weave around each other in shock and alarm. Pregnant women are bending down, releasing their once precious loads, and then joining the moaning, shrieking multitudes. There are wild beasts darting through the startled crowds, and suddenly, recognition… the family members I left so many generations ago come into view. Their necks are cranked upward, and their eyes are fixed in a stone stare, fearful to let an instant go by, not even allowing a blink. They pass by me, knowing we are all beyond help now. The rippling earth seems to have calmed and, as we watch, is expanding into a level plain, flat and unadorned. We stop, riveted in our places as the sun drops to a place directly above our heads. I never thought I would wish to be back in that hellhole of a grave, but that is my most ardent wish now…

DAY OF JUDGMENT

Then will the true promise draw nigh:
Then behold! The eyes of the unbelievers
will fixedly stare in horror: "Ah, woe to us!
We were indeed heedless of this;
nay, we truly did wrong..."
[Qur'an, 21: 97]

IT IS DIFFICULT TO KEEP track of time in this flat, open plain, especially with the unrelenting shafts of heat from the sun so close to us now that they are singeing our hair. As near as I can figure, I've been standing in the same spot, trying to keep from drowning in my own sweat, for a good ten lifetimes. Any comfort from my 'afternoon' on the old earth is a distant memory. My reality now is sobbing, sweating, moaning, and seeing the stark reality on the dust-stained faces around me. We are lined up, row after row, a study in despair. I see lips moving slowly on dark faces, still not able to comprehend their obvious fate. The terror of these dire circumstances is causing anguish and regret, some even swooning and biting down on their hands in fear.

I am trying to find some good I did, some deed I might use in my defense, but everything I did was for myself, and try as I might, I come up empty. I am silently cursing my parents for not showing me the right way. They were far astray with no 'god' but pleasure and comfort, and I followed in their shallow footsteps to my doom. My brooding reflection is interrupted once again by the vision of another 'face of light' being lifted to a cool and shady spot under a beautifully gilded canopy. The mood is bleak at best for us without shelter; our skin raw and chafed from a thousand years of terminal glaring by the sun's piercing rays. How many more years must we stand in this bleary-eyed stupor without a lessening? How can we escape this excruciating, immobile existence? Maybe those we followed in the lifetime have the power to intercede. Where are they? Why don't they come forward in our time of need? I alternate between rage and regret, wanting to blame anyone, everyone…but the truth always comes back to me. No one can bear my burden now. The folly of my short-lived life haunts me every moment, my mind twisting and turning, trying to get away from the truth, but how can you ignore what is blatantly obvious…we are without allies, without the comforting light of goodness, without hope…the grim truth is, we are ruined…

FACING ALLAH

*And to every soul will be paid in full
the fruit of its deeds, and
Allah knows best all that they do…*
[Qur'an, 39: 70]

RESOUNDING THUNDER AND WHAT APPEARS to be shimmering rain explode above us, finally breaking the anguish and monotony of the Day of Reckoning that has held us hostage for 50,000 years. Our heads snap up as rank upon rank of angels begin to descend, filling the expanded horizon with their dazzling numbers, lining themselves up in perfect rows, shoulder to shoulder. There is rejoicing among the 'faces of light', but we of the dark side know this only means our doom is closer. All at once there is a ripple of white light so brilliant it covers the entire space above us. We see a group of the most beautiful angels yet carrying a throne of gold that is radiating goodness, pulsing with the convergent life forms of the heavens and the earth. The Being on the throne is veiled from our sight, but as no truth is hidden this day, we instinctively know it is our Lord. There is a hush as the 'faces of light' drop to their knees and fall forward in prostration. We of the darkness try desperately to join them, but are unable to bend. The desire is strong, but it feels unfamiliar to us. The fear in my throat deepens as I realize my fate is sealed.

I hear a commotion on my left and turn my eyes to behold thousands and thousands of angels in iron bridles, each dragging thousands of chains attached to them. Hoards of these light beings are groaning under the weight of something not quite in view. I begin to feel intense heat throbbing against my skin and the sounds of crackling and hissing fill the air. As the angels strain to move forward, I begin to see sparks the size of camels snapping all around me. I want to look away and run, but my eyes are riveted to the creature at the end of the chains. Its smell precedes it as it churns along its path, and my companions begin to gasp and wheeze, choking on the smoke. This blazing beast is massive and boiling and growling its way toward us, and my heart sinks as I realize this will be my new home. Fire…not just flames, but bubbling black heat so hot it consumes everything it touches. It seems to have lethal, clutching hands coming from everywhere, and we of the dark side are its target. I am reminded of a picture I saw once of a black hole in space; anything coming near it was sucked in, and nothing ever came out again. This is a living, bellowing, sizzling black hole, and I know there is no escaping its grip.

I am vaguely aware that the faces of light are also being shown their new abode. It is green and crisp, fresh with the promise of peace and security, something I don't believe I will ever feel again, and now a new level of remorse and sadness settles into my heart. Through my tears I see some faces of light running from prophet to prophet looking for intercession, eager for the judgment to begin so they can go to their new homes in the Garden, but I fervently hope the accounting never starts. I still wonder how I got in so deep…why couldn't I see…was the deception so deep? Why is this happening to me now?

My confusion becomes even greater when I hear what sounds like a flock of birds in the distance. I perceive what I believe are the flapping of a multitude of wings, but as the sound approaches I see they are not birds, but millions and millions of books, some fat, some thin, and they are soaring overhead. These scrolls begin dropping out of the sky, and what appears to be a random dance is actually a choreographed, judicial declaration, one book deftly landing in each hand. Some hopeful souls have their right hands stretched up to the air and squeal with delight as their book drops neatly into the desired spot. I feel my left arm worm its way behind my back and feel a thump as a book is caught there. I quickly bring the treatise forward, and it pops open to reveal everything I tried to keep hidden in my life, all the dirty deals, cheating, backbiting, times of denial of God, everything. I feel waves of panic as I realize that this book recorded every move I made, every word I uttered, every thought I had. Oh, my God, nothing is left out! How can I defend myself now when the truth is so glaring!

We begin to be called one by one, and when my time comes, I approach the veiled Being with many excuses on my tongue, but as I get closer my mouth becomes stiff and finally snaps shut, sealing forever my defense. I want to offer ransom now, everything I ever owned, my husband, my children, my land, anything…I want to tell Him to put my children in that raging fire instead of me. Every morsel of food, every article of clothing, every piece of gold, I want to bundle it up and extend it forward and beg for mercy, but I have nothing of any value with which to bargain. I struggle to speak as suddenly my hearing finds its voice and begins the litany of sins against its purity - the gossip I listened to, the music spouting out forbidden things, the TV shows that desensitized my heart to true cleanliness and devotion, and the many sources speaking ill of God's religion and His prophets. My eyes and skin also begin their unending inventory of what I focused on and wrongfully touched in my lifetime. It all comes spilling out, poisoning any chance I might have had to try and redeem myself in my Creator's eyes. Despair and hopelessness are my new companions now as I am led back to the waiting crowd of dispirited souls destined for the conflagration. All luster has been sapped from my existence…

THE SCALE

But those whose balance of good deeds is light
will be those who have lost their souls:
in Hell will they abide…
[Qur'an, 23: 103]

I AM SLOWLY BEING MOVED farther and farther away from the faces of light and smoke and ash begin to cover my body. It is hot here, stifling, and I notice the earth around me getting scorched and desolate. Worse than that is the loss of the Divine Light I never acknowledged was there during my whole existence, but sorely miss now. Like a flickering candle, it is ebbing out of me, and a creeping sense of loss and dread is taking its place. Oh, is there no way back? Is there no promise I can make that will be believed? I shudder as the light that gave me my 'human' qualities, virtue, honor, goodness and nobility, withdraws, leaving only flesh and bones with no purpose. Through eyes that can only weep now, I see a golden scale, with two horizontal gold disks suspended with silver rods and gold chains, appear between the two groups of light and dark, and I strain to see the judgment beginning. The faces of light are approaching the scale one by one, watching most of their deeds being loaded on the disk of good on the right. There is euphoria as their few bad deeds are jettisoned into the air by the weight of their good, and their reward seems as certain as the punishment I am getting a taste of now. As the last of the righteous ones is judged and sent on to the next scene in this Day of Inevitable Truth, the condemned group I am in begins their weighing of deeds. This doesn't take long as most of our deeds on earth were done selfishly, and the left side of the scale, where bad deeds are measured, is always heavy, and the right, the place of good deeds, is permanently lacking. Not one of us seems to have any good deeds to save us. Every bad act we ever did is piled on, tiny black seeds of deficiency floating onto the top from everywhere, flecks of useless deeds sown, sealing our fate forever. I see now that justice is complete this day. I sink deeper into despair when I step forward to the scale and see that the left side is spilling over with copious amounts of my empty actions. As an angel raises itself up to announce my shame to humanity, I realize the words professing my failure are the truth. Shame and self-reproach well up in me, and I have nowhere to turn. The fire towers above us now in columns, drawing in its breath and bursting with fury, ready to eat its fill…

THE SIRAT

Such as took their religion to be mere amusement and play and were deceived by the life of the world, that Day shall we forget them as they forgot the meeting of this day of theirs…
[Qur'an, 7: 51]

I AM MOVING NOW, WEARY, my skin charred from the insistent licking of the flames surrounding me. I still have a shred of hope that the worst of this nightmare is behind me as I trudge forward to a flat plain ahead. It seems peaceful enough until I get a little further down the trail. Barely able to put one foot in front of the other, I begin to smell the worst of rotting flesh, open infected wounds, and the wail of high-pitched screams fill the fetid air around me. The source of the foul odor and desperate howls comes into sight as we near the edge of a great pit of smoldering fire and smoke, stretching as far as the eye can see. There is a blade as thin as a hair suspended across this churning pit, and I see some souls filled with light flying across its gleaming edge, some walking gingerly, marking their next step, and some merely limping along, their light flickering, keeping their steps hesitant. There are iron hooks on either side of the blade that seem to make a judgment of their own and many dark souls are caught in their cold grasp, pulled down to be added as kindling for the beast ignited below. I slow down now, pulling back in horror. The only light I have is from the flames as they rise to greet me, calling to me mockingly to join them and the millions of writhing, twisting bodies they already own.

I concentrate now and begin the perilous journey across, all of my senses heightened to the slightest movement and sound. I must rely on my sense of touch to feel this thin footpath, and try to balance as I push ahead. The blackness adds to the terror I feel, and I hear the snapping of the ravenous pincers at my ankles as they wait for any stumble, any misstep on my part. I grit my teeth, determined not to fall, plotting my next move with every muscle of my body. I inch slowly forward, finding a tiny bit of confidence now, hoping that at the end of this I will find some light, some peace, some respite. I make my mind come back from those thoughts immediately, afraid to lose even a second's concentration, but the hope still lingers there like a thought stuck in time, dangling like a blossom on a branch. Suddenly I feel a searing pain in my left ankle as a cold iron hook ensnares it completely. Horrified, I feel my body being dragged off the blade, and I am roughly thrown down, down into the pit, falling for what seems like years, the skin on my body roasting through even before I make contact. Oh! The heat is unbearable, the screams of the damned deafening, and the oozing slime smells like a killing field. As the skin on my body replicates itself, I am adding my agony to the fray, a primal howl that can only touch on the wretchedness I feel. There is no light, only smoke; no fresh air, only squalid fumes of burned and infected bodies. I am only vaguely aware of the hundreds who fell with me as they too begin to voice their suffering. "LET ME OUT!" "PLEASE, LET ME OUT!" "LET IT END!!" But it all falls on deaf ears...

BRIDGE OF QISAS

*The Day when man will see
the deeds that his hands
have sent forth and the unbeliever will say,
Woe to me! Would that I were mere dust!"*
[Qur'an, 78: 40]

I AM TORN FROM MY MOLTEN misery for a moment as I watch with envy the next step for those who believed. The regret is palpable as we of the fire grasp the full meaning of what we are seeing. The faces of light approach a dome-shaped bridge with many people scattered on it separated into pairs. Some are slapping or being slapped; some are being handed gold and some are receiving it; others are exchanging cloth and other goods, and tears are flowing from both sides. This seems to be some sort of final purification for them, the final cleansing to get them ready to enter their new home. I see many animals there, running in the meadow under the bridge. They, too, are getting their payback from the lifetime, and as small birds attack hawks, gazelle are bringing down lions, and rabbits are swallowing snakes whole. As each of the wrongdoings is satisfied and justice is done, my envy knows no bounds as I watch the beasts turn to dust. It is the 'nothing' existence I had imagined my whole life, and now I beg and plead for every agonizing moment. I feel the excruciating pain, as my ever-constant companion, the crackling blaze, sears my skin to the bone and pulls back to admire its handiwork, awaiting the skin's regeneration and the next torment it can inflict. Dust, oh beautiful, peaceful dust! Please take me now…

THE HELLFIRE

Those who desire the life of the present and its glitter,
to them We shall pay the price of their deeds
within, without diminution. They are those for whom
there is nothing in the Hereafter but the Fire...
[Qur'an, 11: 15-16]

I JOIN THE BLACKENED GROUP headed for Malik, the gate-keeper of our smoldering confinement. We beg him to intervene for us to his Lord, as we have been completely cut off from any divine influence. We plead for death if we cannot leave this place. I am past what I can tolerate, and there must be an end to the torment I am enduring. This resolute being looks at us with disgust and says, "Did a warner not come to you?" I feel as if I am going to explode from remorse and shame, and my new body, the skin thickened to increase the suffering, has become an unending source of pain. I frantically implore Malik to ask his Lord to soften the punishment or give us some respite. He tires of us and with a hot iron rod pushes us back to our places, and to a renewal of our just desserts. We are chained to one spot, our garment of fire seared to our skin, and boiling water is poured over our heads that melts us from the outside in. As soon as the anguish of the burning subsides, a new body is formed, and it begins again…and oh, the thirst…I am so thirsty, but all we are given to drink is a boiling fluid composed of the scalded fat and putrid pus from the charred skin continuously being burned off. We gulp down the fetid liquid, but it doesn't quench the thirst. I am choked by the black smoke that clings to my body like a thick fog. Sometimes I think I am getting used to the level of extreme torture, but then I sense it becoming worse. I am scorched from above and below, and all around me is a heat hotter than any seventy fires felt in the lifetime. Some days we are brought forth in wretched groups to a twist-ed and seething tree called Zaqqum on the lowest and hottest level of our humiliating abode. We are forced to drink liquid like molten brass that makes our insides boil like a caldron of oil. We reach to pick the fruit hanging from this vine of venom, but this most damned of provisions is shaped like the head of demons, and our thirst is antagonized to a degree beyond toleration from the bitter taste. When we have finished drinking this acrid swill, we are sent back to our chains and the grueling abuse begins all over again. It never lessens; there is no light except the glow of the walls kindled for thousands of years to a white heat, and the air clogs our lungs with its grating dust.

To add to my misery, a window to the Garden is opened to me and my companions, and we are shown our homes there, where we could have been had we only believed and recognized our Creator. We must endure visions of stunning gardens with cool rivers flowing beneath them, the beaming residents wearing the finest of clothing as they eat the most succulent of fruits, and sip the most tantalizing of liquids. I call out to them, "Oh, can you give me some of that sweet elixir," but I no sooner make the request and a wall appears between us. I can see on their side of the barrier great peace and contentment, and on my side only darkness and degradation. I cry out and try to bargain to get the punishment lightened by telling all the good deeds I did in my lifetime- the charity, the kindness, the good words I spoke- but I am reminded that I did all that to be called generous, and I got my reward in my time on earth. I am reminded that I sent nothing ahead for the Hereafter, and never even believed there was life after death, so why should I expect to be rewarded here. Resignation is added to the long list of emotions I embody in my new life, and the fire seems to have just gotten a little hotter…

The years of torment drag on, with no end in sight. I have lost my time frame and can't even remember one moment of good I had in my short time on earth. We are continually subjected to new and more extreme forms of torture by our fiery captor, and this fiendish beast, the Hellfire, is stronger than ever. A few souls who believed, but were evil, have been forgiven after they pay their debt, and are pulled out from around us, adding to our grief, as we of the hopeless give up any hope of hope.

In one particularly painful moment, the window to the Garden is opened, and we see all of the blessed inhabitants gathered in the central market, waiting. We watch in trepidation as a giant ram is brought in front of the crowd, and we listen to the announcement coming from their Lord. I have waited eons for any shred of good news, of respite from this daily conflagration, and I listen anxiously to see if this might be the day I am freed. The words I hear next rip out my heart and the last of my hope with it. This ram represents death and will be slaughtered, making an end to death itself, thus sealing my fate forever in this place of misery and dejection. If I thought I couldn't feel any worse, I was wrong. When the knife slices through the beast's jugular, my anguish laments. No release, no salvation, never a ray of light to be seen…for all time. As the fire roars in victory, I scream with lips burned and displaced, "Oh, would that death would have made an end of me…"

SOURCES

The Holy Qur'an

The authenticated sayings of the Prophet Muhammad
(Peace be upon him)

Death & Dying by Ahmed H. Sakr, PhD

"What does the spirit do in the grave?"
www.islamanswers.net

Numerous lectures sourced from
the Holy Qur'an and sayings of the Prophet

———————————